Has the illusion of personal history and its
succinct than in these poems? "Occasion: / l:
long poem, "The Leniad," takes Virgil's Aeneid   ...epic that famously
begins, "I sing of arms and the man"—and allows "the man" (here, named Leni instead
of Aeneas) to speak for himself. When Leni talks about "arms," he's talking not about
armor and spears but about "the arms of a man." These poems revel in the delight of
thinking, of writing, of language, of love, and of being brought down and built back
up (like Rome from the ashes of Troy) after a break up. They are nothing short of
remarkable, the kind of fun that makes you think.

— Mary Jo Bang, *A Film in Which I Play Everyone*

The Leniad takes inspiration from Virgil, from Dante, but *The Leniad* is like nothing
else, its scope both epic ("*...the last time I made this trip/ into the lower level of hell/the
cliff face hadn't yet collapsed*") and momentary ("the worried look of something about
to turn in a wind"). This is an exhilarating journey, the frozen past and the grim here-
and-now liberated, enlivened by discourse, intercourse, their astonishing offspring,
poems both wildly inventive and brainy, erotically charged and heart-breaking. In the
hands of the cerebral cortex, heartbreak sparkles.

— Kathryn Davis, *Aurelia, Aurélia*

"A little edge / was there, to put / his foot on." In even the smallest moves of erotic
self-consciousness that motivate and score these poems and sequences, Nathaniel
Rosenthalis recalls how gods in antiquity would engineer propitious conditions where
men's desire wanted encouragement. If there is a ledge, a leverage, a favorable light,
a volta, a vantage, this poet's line will find it and savor its glimmer, against loss and
caution and the world's contingency. The hero of *The Leniad* has been equipped and
delivered, without escape, to "Lust, that bluish type of situatedness." No one said he
couldn't take notes.

— Brian Blanchfield, *Proxies*

PRAISE FOR NATHANIEL ROSENTHALIS

"My devotion, after all/is that I even got up," says Nathaniel Rosenthalis, belying the title of his mesmerizing debut, *I Won't Begin Again*. For, in poem after poem, Rosenthalis argues for – and enacts – resilience in a world where doubt can seem "the architecture of the moment." "Not fantasizing, not hoping, was error also," and indeed these poems resist the world's (and the self's) instability by noticing the least detail ("it was like/resistance//to notice, so/I did. And do") but through a teetering of vision: a green wall is "millionly leafy," the sun "crumples one random can," which is to say that the poems are acts of reinvention, of reimagining life's possibilities. Philosophical, surreal in the tradition of Rimbaud's *Illuminations*, and slyly erotic, *I Won't Begin Again* is finally a triumph of emotion, what Rosenthalis defines as "putting yourself over another/to make a different sense." I feel changed by these poems – powerfully so, gratefully.

— Carl Phillips, *Then the War*

A poetics of localized intense being—no, a poetics of intensive being, localized at one point to "an arm movement whose flipside is my tender wrist," at another to "a tiara floating." Nathaniel Rosenthalis writes less of what one does daily and more of what one *is*, the *thus* of what one is, distilled, malty, vialed up—then spilled. OK. I love these poems; that's simpler to say but doesn't get at the "deadpan glamor" of this poet's very particular kind of (un)canny—it's both—grammar and mordant enjambment ("Be redundant / to a shamefastness / you were // made real through") which, enthralled, I heed.

— Aditi Machado, *Emporium*

They say *timing is everything*. I can't remember what they say that about. Romance? Language? In Nathaniel Rosenthalis' *I Won't Begin Again*, *timing is everything* is true for just about everything. From mis-overhearing small profundities on the street to 'the motion of coming down a stair,' Rosenthalis shows that our inescapable timelines are beautiful and lonely and funny. In 'A Ten-Minute Moment' he slows time and guides us through that sparkling carelessness with which we first turn over an hourglass to the antsy loss we feel watching the last grain of sand fall to the bottom. He writes with an easy, abstract humor: 'I am often,' he says in a poem called 'On Where I'm Not Supposed to Exist.' He writes with a boundarylessness between the 'I' and all that is outside it: 'A newspaper blows across the hardwood floor, making me want to be held. I write down "Behold."' These poems highlight the way the world works its constant absurdity and they help us feel okay when we realize we work that same way. A dangerous desire, love, and intimacy ripple through the poems: 'how / hot it was when // he slammed what / a door had been, for him. / Into me.' I get that. Damn do I get that—to feel most alive when loved and loving. It stops the clock for a moment."

— Sommer Browning, *Good Actors*

Nathaniel Rosenthalis's poems have a beguiling transparency and simplicity that serve as winsome screen for the complications provided by his syntax and his emotional orientation toward curlicue, paradox, and detour. Morsels of keen portraiture verging on abstraction, sometimes seeming like expressionist dramas rendered in clean cut-outs, Rosenthalis's cameos occupy the prose-poem terrain of Charles Simic, Anne Carson, and Max Jacob, with a warm debt to Gertrude Stein's angular defamiliarizations. I'm instantly drawn into Rosenthalis's imaginative world and I want to stay there forever.

— Wayne Koestenbaum, *Figure It Out*

What an amazing range of language!—but no matter how far out it goes, it always lands exactly right. And right in the middle of the infinitesimal moments that actually determine human relationships—the glance back, the sudden laugh, the walking down a stair—Rosenthalis finds the precise points at which people actually connect. An uncanny intuition leads both form and content to fuse with a certainty that rings and a compassion that radiates throughout.

— Cole Swensen, *On Walking On*

Not just insight, but the strange detours consciousness must take to know itself--"I'm interested in the edge/I strive toward;" not just desire, but the strange ways it flashes in and out of time; there's no one writing quite like Rosenthalis. "Buscando ser más," said Paulo Freire, and this is poetry that demands more, from experience, the self, the poem itself. A deep sense of responsibility to the art shines through.... This is an extraordinary debut.

— D. Nurkse, *A Night in Brooklyn*

John Ashbery wrote of Jennifer Bartlett, whose *Air: 24 Hours* paintings inspired the breezy poems in Nathaniel Rosenthalis's *24 Hour Air*, that it was her habit "to begin with a basic concept and work it out *ad absurdum*, ultimately sabotaging its 'purity' with freewheeling improvisation." The same applies here, where the sensuousness of the quotidian is released from the day's regimen, attaining the measured extravagance of, say, mirrors, liriopes, and, why not, expansive towels. Like the day's events, the phrases and images in these poems repeat and recombine now and then, reminding us that regularity doesn't preclude our daily extemporizing but rather delimits its boundaries. Read this work and wonder, again, why the day can't have more than twenty-four hours.

— Mónica de la Torre, *Repetition Nineteen*

THE LENIAD

Nathaniel Rosenthalis is the author of *The Leniad* (Broken Sleep Books, 2023). His debut book of poems, *I Won't Begin Again*, won the 2021 Burnside Review Press Book Award, selected by Sommer Browning. His poems have appeared in *Granta*, *The Chicago Review*, *New American Writing*, *Lana Turner*, *The Harvard Advocate*, *Denver Quarterly*, *Conjunctions*, and elsewhere. Based in New York City, he teaches writing at NYU and Columbia University and also works as an actor and singer.

Also by Nathaniel Rosenthalis

I Won't Begin Again   (Burnside Review, 2023)

24 Hour Air   ([Pank], 2022)

The Leniad

Nathaniel Rosenthalis

Broken Sleep Books

ISBN: 978-1-915760-28-9

Cover designed by Aaron Kent & Joe Kent

Edited & Typeset by Aaron Kent

Broken Sleep Books Ltd
Rhydwen
Talgarreg
Ceredigion
SA44 4HB

Broken Sleep Books Ltd
Fair View
St Georges Road
Cornwall
PL26 7YH

Contents

The Leniad

Machoville

The sex in my books is never merely hot.
— Dennis Cooper

Byzantium

Once, I had a mother and a father.
To both of them I was a little tug boat. The waters were real waters.

Then one went away. The other was wetter.
Splashed upon, minus the ritual cleaning, that water.

Of all forms I've taken, some might say only the human matters.
I in my garden. I miss out on some looping vines. The pale green buds to water.

About Being Cold

A man called today
and said he's my
father. Being quasi-
myself, I had no other.
Couldn't only eye
the one guy's car.
Door opens, an orange
light slices.
Even more men
came down the steps,
invited by the hammer-
ing of the one
to watch.
Feeling got out.
Getneighborly.com.
He was dead, my father.
Incredibly of
the down road.
Just occurring birds
were talking but
not to me. "Kill me now
I just about died."
Latecomer outcome.
My giving more is
then getting moved.
No, one will. Oh but
they're birds, I thought,
as if I didn't know.
Poetry would say
"if doubt is your man, get / on
your knees, you / night
// socket." Quiet.

Robins know
to land. Squirrels,
branch.
The perpetual present.
Uncertain waves again.
Versus a cloud I sometimes am
and people are, passing
under me.
We're each other.
X is for the concrete
I can also be, like sidewalk
under them.
You needn't halo anyone
is all I hear.
Zeroes'll round you out.

"Of His Mistrisse upon Occasion of Her Walking in a Garden"

is the title of a sonnet by one
Henry Constable who is the lover,
the man, Shakespeare is in love with in
his *Sonnets*. This would be a good title
to repurpose for my poem if I
wanted to be the long lost lover
who did exist, whom people deny
as such did. Do. Will. This would not be
a good title to repurpose if I worried
for a long-gone past that didn't even cross
its own real hairs; I wouldn't catch, not
being of scruffy beard, readiness to pose
for a portrait capturing a likeness
and now hands, and hangs in Room 321
in the Metropolitan Museum of
Art in New York, New York. This would be a
good title to repurpose if I were bent
on paying attention to a problem
that pokes me in the face when I sniff it.
Namely, those are lilies. This would not be
a good title to repurpose this would
not be a title this would not be a
good to a purpose for my poem for
my poem. "Constable's modern editor
Joan Grundy says she has searched all British
and Continental poems and can find
no other instance of a violet ac-
quiring its color by being soaked in blood."
(Scarry 63) This makes me wonder
to history for examples of what
it might, after all, be like
if this title would be good re: the

16

purpose of seeing a poem depend
on us who, historically naive or
not, have never been in love

Ovid

Unless you're the
one I turn to to feel safe, or a rush. Matrices
      of isolation.
Oh, like you said, worst case scenario is I know.

A Visit to Hades

included a
yelping grovel
-ing type, taking
up his ass a
frozen white shape.
I made him. I
the bearish
man. Didn't
tell him how to
contemplate
it. Make him ec-
static. I told him lick.
He did. Could for
one two hits. The
drip congealed.
A little edge
was there, to put
his foot on. Test-
ing testing the
drop-off zone

Sappho

When many a guy seeks out
the first-person I, the moment becomes Aphrodite, who
if you stayed here five years and kept on asking
how many things the fighters suffered there
to get off, period, they see a
Sappho to Sappho herself, who has now
you, would get bored and go back home, again
attractive, guy they want to fuck, him
become the second-person you
when they watch

Teotihuacan and Us

The one in blue and white horizontal stripes is me, with a friend on my left, a friend on my right. We're holding our phones high, aiming the distance back at a site. A ziggurat, surrounded by lesser (?) ziggurats. We may be ourselves on a ziggurat. I forget. The sky is whitish over the mountains but a darker blue the higher-up we look. So we do. Sean is stuck on the sublime. Vince is too much a sucker-stickler for stand-alone clarity. I'm the one who shivers, inserting some quip about no one yet fingering my newby beard. We're all in backwards baseball caps, but I'm sad now. Using these words, stiffening the brush. But it's not sadness I feel at the height of that. Bristles in the wind.

Sycophantism

     Public as a butterfly
broach your great self said was a good idea to pin on your
coat

Another Swan

I'm right
on the steps of a
hall. Hubris.
It helped the
heaving of having
been there in some
same past. That is all
where I lived, for
my changes. Sky
neutral and bone-
ready. I was ready. A boy
bluffed he wasn't.
I couldn't change
pronounishly. Oh
I hummed him but
can I be fluent
about myself. About
the plus or minus
light of day I do this in.
And am there for.

The Leniad

If we boil down the story, we're left with a few bare bones. Leni eats at a restaurant with an ex. Travels on a bus between cities. Has a hotel hookup, or three. Importantly, for our purposes, he keeps a journal.

I

A dove
is no omen.
Not of a man
on the lookout for Dad.

A man we'll call Leni
faces a couple
on a patio.
An attempt at order.

An observer, he
faces the other:
"I'm not just an outsider,
I wear low green shoes. Militarily. If I

appear nostalgic, using faddish forms, look again at the emoji bag
at my feet. I close my hooded eyes."

An appearance
he'd chosen
to embody bodied him.

"Are you sure
the flight of names
isn't in air
by default?"

As if asking the bus driver.
Driver doesn't hear.
Girl with late braids approaches at the next stop.
Gets on.

At least he is not just in his mind: he sees her blue zip-up.
Ergo erstwhile worthwhile warmth.

"Coming!" yells his intel.
Up goes a ball
of smushed duct tape the girl throws.
Not looking at him.

He knew
people saying they are dead
already were.

He knows about his current man:
"His tongue will probably
flicker too fast again in my mouth
like a bad light.
I'll shut my eyes and hold tight and fall.
Go nowhere
and split. The end." He writes this down.

"Eyes flash." "Eyes flash." "The eyes of an unfaithful lover look just like a trapped dog's." "Eyes glow when a god feels warmth." "Eyes glow when a god is about to scheme." "To have the eyes of an owl, fly and be a goddess." "Your eyes are horn or ivory when you try to stay unbreakable, when your heart is busy breaking."

Here is Dante's *Inferno*, open by his hand:
I want you to know the last time I made this trip
into the lower level of hell
the cliff face hadn't yet collapsed.

"I would be buried.
Being buried feels like the past.
A sequence!
Since I'm only here, whoever isn't
isn't my friend.
Hope is stillness in a choir
and I hope not in tears."

In the long afterlife of having been in a couple,
he was obvious. Ready
for his next one. He briefed himself often to that end.

"Is coming to ask
what deserving is?"
This, from the Latest X. He blinks back.

Occasion:
last Friday.
Still bitter.

That mirror. He checks his tongue
to see orange.
"Infection?" said internet.
"Could be," he thought.
He'd been precious in the perspective
of pretending to preach:

"You can't say I don't talk about tenderness.
You can't always look back at the sun you know."

Nature is not there
to be asked from forever. Nonetheless
Leni asks: "I know that I love
and to do so requires abiding, into which everybody falls at least once."

Often he isn't present.
He thinks a man
would be easy to love "if
only if."

Often he snaps back into a place he is in.
"So name your preferred time to wake up with eyes that flutter
open only
to see your last love close."

Or: "Maybe don't space out your days anymore
so that you are mistakable for a vacuum cleaner."

"The heart is made of iron." "The heart is a bed." "The heart is someone who gives commands." "The heart is a monitor to be read." "The heart is a detective, and has suspicions." "The heart is for eating, so put it on a plate." "The heart breaks." "The heart is a blessing that comes into being when you welcome a stranger." "You might think that the heart is solid: all the more reason it melts." "The heart can yap, whimper, bark, just as a dog, but especially a mama dog, the forcible entirety of her little ones she can't let go of when a stranger comes too close." "The heart is a dog that other dogs go after." "The heart has the squirming motions of sausages in a hot skillet." "The heart is harder than a rock." "The heart is iron."

Picture a set of shapes.
He makes them and
flows into
only those shapes.

Sexual Personae by Camille Paglia is open by his hand: *promiscuity*
in men
may cheapen love
but sharpen thought.

The difference is when he sees a pigeon,
he doesn't scare it off.
It is its lot.

"The door behind me clicks.
A door is more like me than not."
Sound: it's an obligation.

"Then I should learn to drive.
I'll pass anyone.
They won't stare at me again."
He is still on the bus.
"When do they, other people,
get to be that way, content with their lot?
And why?"

To no longer be a child, have one
was a punchline.
He heard it on a TV show his mother recommended.
The set-up:
to begin again, like a bed,
wait any morning like a pillow, instead of a head.

"Grief wraps around you, eats your heart." "Grief is a woman who falls upon her husband, dead from battle in protection of his home and offspring, or who isn't dead yet, and is gasping, and so she wails, falling again on his form, even as enemy soldiers encroach on her, putting the tips of their swords on her, beginning the journey of the new widow into harder life." "Grief is hungry for a heart." "Grief keeps its own private measuring system." "Grief is a bed you roll around in." "Grief is a weight that can go on you, like a blanket, and blankets keep you warm." "Grief is a bed you sleep in sometimes." "Grief is a big man who overwhelms you." "Grief is a black cloud that can wrap itself."

Today
will not change
its logos
like on a shirt.

"That's not my real name."

We know, Leni.
Westin. Super8. Aloft. Starbucks.
Baltimore aquarium ("60 miles away!").
Those are real names.
They repeat as necessary.

You can only show grief
pours its two handfuls of ashy dust
upon you
many times.

II

A scant metaphysics
is scatterable. A man put his hand
on Leni's ankle.
"I'll yes myself," Leni thinks. As per usual.

"As a man, it's not that I struggle to think about magic or blood"
says the Latest X.
The two of them are munching at a restaurant table.
Cold night.
He zooms inward.

"Again is one gift
of fewer sexual partners."
He looks in the bathroom mirror.
Availability
makes him often gathering.

Blowback.
Leni passes a center
for conventions, side-eyeing
the suits in and out.
A long line. "It's as if a lone
line has a static
I absorb, and I need it."

Convention subject: porn.
Porn can't be separated from art. *Great art
is always flanked by its dark sisters, blasphemy and pornography* (says a pull-out
quote).

"Desire's eventual."
He thinks this, in this city.
"How much is rent?"

"A man is a force, but feeling defeated, his eyes will burn like fire, bright, not dim, as he comes upon pretty local girls, who are like cows or sheep in sturdy pens, because he is a mountain lion." "A man is the in-taking of a breath by a god; when the god gives him mouth to mouth, the man gets good at words." "A man is a giant who supersedes comparison with the usual types that live on bread; compare him to the wooden peak in airy mountains." "A man is a lion at home on a mountain when he eats." "A man looks like fish when speared." "A man is a pig in a landlord's feast when he's one of many murdered." "A man is a prince who tends to be young, with the soft skin." "A man is a young boy who grew up like a tree to match limb for limb that dropped seed." "A man is material to begin." "A man is a boy who glows like embers." "A man is a goose when he's one of many, gathering to waste wealth." "A man is trash when he puts his feet up to get nasty." "A man who talks too much is an old woman at work on an old oven." "A man who takes up space in the minds of many, that's a hero." "A man is a god when more than one honors him." "A man is non-existence if you can't prove him."

Doing love well is will.
He looks outside his apartment building.
It's cold.
He mis-sings, *We ain't ever getting older with our roommates back in Boulder.*

"For why shouldn't I roll.
My eyes do me.
To do as done and still to do.
Change no wet blue jeans, take no

hat off in the wind, for an answer."
He hears a ringing alarm of a car
and calls it violation.
No such thing as noticing no small thing.

He's getting out of jeans.
This opens his mouth.

He's aware
inhaling faster thru the nose
when you suspect a bad smell
is rude.

"I'd laugh.
His musk is like the gasoline
Dad used to power his boat.
He died when I was nine. Death happens then spring's back." He writes this down.

"I crave danger
sometimes. Then I go back to the selfsame green.
The green iPod I wrap the
flat headphone cords around."

Into the huge day he rides, on a train.
Hears the highway is blue in a blur. "I listen."

"He's not mine. Nor are his hands
mine now
which he had folded me up
with."

"If not, one attends," Leni thinks.
He is looking up
at loud clouds, in a group of buds.
Compare this impression to "She maintained this contradiction."

"I've heard it said 'Who are your parents?'
is one of the most important questions.
You can ask."

Knocking around with them
he looks up at the sky.
No eagle.

"The mind can be injured, or have always lacked the ability to stand up on its own." "The mind is a bodybuilder who has his push-pull routines and thinks he doesn't need rest days." "The mind can craft an outline by rising and falling." "A mind is like a chair that a god can turn to face a new direction, but then that chair can fall apart and you become its pieces." "The mind is a pool whose waters whirl."

"I'm a shop.
The glass display.
First look at the glass, not at your reflection.
Or don't I look past?"

Nature's of the rock sometimes.
"Above the surface, efforts
are under way."
He has this need to know to be.

"Nobody knows anybody.
I enjoy pointing
and I enjoy the same exclusivity of no one else
knowing me."

On a crosswalk in the industrial
downtown of New Jersey, the sun is onto him.

"To park my truck
at night on the street.
To see a sniveling spotlight.
Navel swiveling."

"Too this is our life
and we did live it"
is his meaning.
The extraordinary pure regret moving through the front door of his apartment.

Top-down idealism, like a condom.
"But I told him no fucking.
He gave me two loads: in between
we talked." He is assessing this or that

truth there is to a given.
Freedom is that ongoing unlocking, like eyes.

"Night is a fabric that stretches from heaven." "Night is an object that falls from up above." "Night is a description of the way a dead hero walks." "Night is what falls through the bitter moonlessness." "Night is a pitch." "Night has hands enough to wrap you up." "Night is an interpretation of the inside of a house, in the mind of a man who doesn't know better."

Unclear, on time,
he looks at a few words, like
"scapegoat."
On his way to work he saw

wheat stalks, waving
in the way a willow does, all of them fenced
by a mall, a few hotels plopped
and a clearance spelled out — 14' 3"

where "vitalism," he thinks,
isn't a roundaboutness.
He isn't beyond coming undone.

"You're not here, but I wear an infinity scarf.
At my best, I am unlike a bird.
I don't eat to breed."

With people around, he changes. "Oh so is shame
my problem. But I'm possible to know
like a woven coat. There is that
itch factor

you know." He's a tone on his big red bed.
A piece of the moment is cut
by the lack
of a knife he holds.

"You shouldn't,"
he says, "fasten
yourself."

What depth is
is slow, like pain
to restrict outpouring sound.

III

A shadow passes him.
It speaks:
"I am missing from you the impact of your sex."
That's one approachment.

A surplus is a piece of wind
that fate put in.
He has cut back on his body.
Can't not.

"Be obvious."
He layers his scrapings
to make some coat
to carry him through.

"But the average and the cute sustain me." He writes this down, looks out.
Prudential Center is announced by a tiny purple sign.

Comparison is a neighborhood.
He's in it.
A curling up a cat does to
invite touch.

Darkness
is a 24/7 place
sketching an eye of a woman.
He sees the longest lashes snow would settle for.

"Doing context isn't meaning alone."
He writes this down.
"Context is my life," snaps the air.
"I know." Switching to a blue pen.

Every window opens
the outside.

"Feeling is a
singularity, but also the foldable couch
of that, laid out," he thinks
on a mustard yellow one.

Hand gestures of a woman
as a man
does them and the holding of his dog
close to the chest: "These are two ways to feel about

his voice
on my neck."
He writes this down.
The feeling enunciates him.

"I love the form of the dispossessed because I am."
Or wasn't last night's dinner a joke when he said that, out loud.

"Sleep is a substance that falls on your eyes." "Sleep is a substance that has to be poured." "Sleep is a substance that pours." "Sleep is a military man, and conquers all." "Sleep is a sweetener that isn't artificial." "Sleep is a substance that pours on your eyes, from the hands of a god." "When sleep melts off your eyes, you awaken." "Sleep is a fabric that wraps around you." "Sleep is a gift that a god gives your eyes." "Sleep is a gift that you accept after your fill of food with a faithful friend and a family, around a fire." "Sleep is someone who comes and goes." "Sleep is a substance that pours down like a sweet syrup." "Sleep is so wet that it is a downpour, it drenches your eyes." "Sleep is someone who takes control, someone you hire to help you relax and release." "Sleep is a permit signed by a god." "Sleep is a deliverable." "Sleep is a soft washable sheet." "Sleep is a sweet jailer of the heart."

"I glare on
the head-down walkways.
Stores with personal names like Aaron's or Freddy's."
He writes this down.

"I love porn," says a woman
crossing him from behind
Avenue A.
"Nature's heart is at work beneath not being alone."

"I came away
from all that."
"I'm long from such allowance."

In a scarce sacred medium moment, much like this will come to him.
Another joke he tells himself: "Hi mysticism."

"Knowing Antonioni
didn't mean he knew *L'Avventura*."
He writes this down.
"Bossy facefucking then he let me shower."

Luckily all he has
to feel is
magnetized. Behind him, wooden tables in a set-up.

"My body
warms to the type of union
I experience.
Clouds minus disdain.
No vaulting sun is
intent on
honeyed grass."

"Wind is a person who attacks from all directions, and each direction is its own person, so the south hurls, the north grabs, the east yields to the west, who drives it." "Every wind has a place to get to." "A wind can be your best friend, or frenemy." "Some winds belong to robbers, and snatch." "A wind is devious enough to make a trap for men."

"O face of him."
He writes this down.
Goes blank.
"He goes blank."

On-and-off again power generators along the highway
are "brazen soldiers."
Now he's speechifying.
He's small.

Once, pondering an origin
felt a little willful.
"Even as I did, once, look at a begonia
out of a window of a cross-town bus, I have to stop myself

or grab me when I tell or when I won't."
Mount Laurel's next. "I've just woken up."

Or he is a car
if a car could cringe.
"I'm what it is to be totaled."
He writes this down.

Others
pass and make remarks
about his long coat being purple
as he goes.

Outer space
is purple
and in his way.

Representation
is everywhere.
He turns, like a start-up, for a fee.

Say, a bush outside an office.
The pin in a poem that ends as if on one leg: "What I'm trying to
                  say is that it wasn't lonely."

"Words fly." "Words fly out." "Words are wings." "Words are to be weighed." "Words have wings to take." "Words produce their own product, called sense, which persons can agree or disagree on." "Words fly out from a person or a god, either way, equipped with wings." "Some ways of speaking are quite roomy, offering space for information that makes you look good." "Words can receive a kingdom through a lovely headband." "Words fly out of a mouth." "Words fly faster when amazement is around." "Words fly back to a speaker." "A word can soften a listener only sometimes." "Words fly out and out." "Words fly out, your words gain wings when you face someone else." "Words become like feathers when a god is about to speak with a smile in their voice." "Words have wings when your eyes shine." "Words fly when they are headed home." "Words fly out with enough force to break through tears." "Words possess wings when you use them with the purpose of summoning someone somewhere." "A god is someone who uses their words at the right time." "Words are beings with wings, and how many do you think there are of those?" "A word is for obeying." "Words are levers: when you operate them right, grief becomes itself inside a listener, like a balloon." "Words fly from father to son, son to father." "Words still do their framing thing in the head of a man who just lost his head." "Words are quivering and winged for a desperate someone." "Words are fluent in themselves, not each other." "Words have wings sometimes." "Words fly fast when you learn the good news your one love is back." "Words are sharp, so they can be cut." "Words have wings that help them move faster than you think." "Words fly out, but what about in?" "Each word steals a pair of wings for itself."

Since any feeling is a moment
beside its rib,
trust is there.
Polished horn. Or ivory.

Slimmer, he thinks:
"And haven't I been missing
some sort of heart before, or a hat?"
Distance from people makes him feel small.

Squatter, he thinks:
"I'm like that last stair that curves around
an oil reservoir
on the highway's side." "I'm this weird fortunate arm

to a larger structure." "I'm equipped."
"Obnoxious." "I have to answer from that equipage, not for."

"To live without this rhythm."
"To see some spring." "I forget black birds in small groups."
"The air."

"To see again, you have to stop." He's stopped
into his local endless
grocery.
"I was used to this." Picking up an apple, he recalls

two roommates walking in, joshing.
All the joking there is
is between them.
"Like any surface play of light, which is a

view only lasting a few seconds." "I'll remember
that's the sense of even who I am." He thinks this. By the butter.

The World

"What if I wrote a book called *The World*? Impossible. The cover design would have to be likewise. The font would be regular — Times New Roman — but the size so large, the letters wouldn't fit. You'd open the book and flip through. Even then, *The World* would be an inkling unless you know about the copyright page. You'd see the title in 12 font Times New Roman — no, maybe Helvetica! Could I be so bold?— plus other useful info. The publishing body. Subjects. Tags. A sequence of numbers know-how-havers could have. To do so, however, they'd turn from the book. Look elsewhere. Keep moving."

It Happens, So I Fall

The snow I just shoveled I had to stop cuz it made a
scraping too loud for nearby Mom. Her
special ed students are miles away but
via internet are near, can hear. The scraping put me
off too. Even the pix, the pick axe I used gave me relief, and
physical effort can't stop mattering.
Mom ("Did you go outside
yet to feel the cold air? I missed the snow last year…")
is putting her feelers onto   ·
someone else's life. Whenever I hear, I'm near a structure that matters,
and it's no

circular
structure. The snow is still outside and will be, because
it was. So why not be trapezoidal, thinking
I happen, so it falls.

Dead Would

Bring me a sloth. Not the branch the sloth clings to extra dark. Bring me
the close-up of the rat I saw before. Leaving you, its tail now seems like a
genuine part of him. Bring me the dog you put a pink hat on. You laughed
and the dog looked back. Bring me the woods when I think about it, so I
think about it. A softening retreating shape. Like a foremost rabbit I don't
even need to touch.

Virgil

Just like a snake a bronze wheel crushes on the road
an offshoot or overgrowth of them, I see
       or one smashed by a traveler's cruel stone:
that bush, so the overgrowth becomes a home that any
       mangled and half-dead, it's desperate
one with wings can use, claim, customize, occupy, add
       to, glad, glide away but can't. It keeps coiling
bits to make it on your own. Not sure why
       its long body, fiercely rearing up, its neck
the goal. Even a haircut has to converge
       hissing, eyes like fire; but the maimed part drags
with something else we've seen before,
       down, and the snake weaves knots and falls back,
so loneliness doesn't seem to apply. The lone
       on itself: so the ship limped under oars.
Twig doesn't raise an eyebrow. My eyebrow
       still, it spread full sails and reached the port.

The Second He

"Don't be so careful," Dan said to me, the second he
slammed the blue hatchback's back down.
The speed he picked up, from there to here, became a demo.
I liked to play the footage back:
I was withstanding (I was grieving
the disappearing he was doing) that life, because of how
we were together. The same shut-eyed look
his face became when he walked away, in sun-
light, following a line.

"Maybe all I have to be's myself more strange and
true," I said, in a mirror
manner. It was early spring. The magenta snow shovel leaned against
the white railing. A yellow one, better, sturdier,
with range, also. It was like early spring. "Same
thing." Like a bad faith actor at the end of his line. "Maybe
maybe not." The slow local flora and
fauna didn't belong then. I opened my eyes.
Pieces of the words disappearing all the
time. The show of shoes. "Careful." Car-ful.

Hoping for an Opening

Hard rain hurts the neck, which is that soft. A part
to cut. Not to be so grim
and guillotine-gullible, but I have been; safe-
ty, thank you, operates heavy.
Craning backwards, I was warned of bags, big time debris
liable to fall on me ("as if only"). But I report now
back to you, soft
bands everywhere for falling onto, like hard
rain.

Machoville

And when, with gladness in his face, he placed
his hand upon my own, to comfort me,
he drew me in among hidden things.

— Dante

I

I was striding toward a new place, a project for a forest, in a T-shirt that said, "Earn It: The Iron Paradise." Even though I wore that shirt as a joke, I struggled to put aside that narrative. I eyed Dan's back. Lust can mix equal parts with envy, the way rain gives its equal part to soil for stuff to grow, a basic of God's green earth. Dan, with music in his ears. I imagined a robed choir swaying just for him. Part of me said "No" and another part "Do it" re: asking him to be in the moment that was increasingly not forever. I was in the earlier midpoint of the first two thirds of my life, where Dan's company seemed like a balm for cruelty I'd felt and given equally. Dan pointed up ahead with an earbud: "This way is it." A harder dark nipped at his white Nikes.

II

Dan pulled out his phone to show off a portrait of his latest X: "It's hard to get the shadowy anatomy right when I work without a reference." Dan's crooked nose enchanged, no, enchanted me. Shorts on, his long toned legs scrolled. One sneaker higher than the other on a rock. He pinched the stick-figure to make it small, then spread his fingers on the screen to blow it up: "It was his underarm sweat stains and the uneven pattern of his facial hair that did it for me." My eyes didn't adjust to the dense, or trees. I was difficult. Lust, that bluish type of situatedness. The worried look of something about to turn in a wind.

III

"Your ass is pronounced by your pants like a word is by a mouth I can't stop mouthing," said Dan. He snapped my pic. (Its vanishing point comes later: in the background, a beer bottle throws its surface and some clouds are catching and green barely backs some bare leaves.) A thought so small I confused it with a snake: "Everybody does that." The snake could be here and I'd look up nothing about local native species. The snake would become one species and I another, each a set of brackets for beings withstanding nothingness by staying where we are. "So silence happens," I almost said. Off trailed Dan.

IV

The lake was empty. That lake's charisma was its being there, and deep. "I need to piss," said Dan. I laughed then kneeled then opened my mouth. His shrug was a force I couldn't know until that acting. We took off our mesh shirts. Lay in text, each other's grass. I knew I needed to "re-interrogate" (Dan's phrase) what I expected from an action sequence, so I put my shirt back on. A high blue sky is all knowledge that one day will disappear. Being now, I found that hard to swallow. He liked it when I did.

V

Let's skip to where I dared. By putting my left foot on a higher ledge in the bathroom and turning my neck this way then that in front of a mirror, I got a glimpse of my ass. Roses are planted in beds and roses were my father's favorite. Two examples of how I stayed at myself. A mirror only. Dan was in the other room, so in I hopped. "That was epic," he said after, rolling over. Like experience does, over everyone.

VI

In the park, Dan put his curly-haired head on his own crossed arms. I made a prediction about the thickening his middle would do in years. It had its own dynamic, so I was curious. Moreover, I toed no fault line in myself that I couldn't recreate. Dan didn't snore. Someone who's never painted faces well before gets a sense of ease when told there are several in a scene, and so draws strength, even conviction, from painting the faces different from one another. That's how I went around. Some people were on bikes, not oppressing the leaves. Some were at the edge of the fake lake, putting on lotion.

VII

I took Dan to a plastic garden. In it, we were like the fuzz a drain catch-es. No water will flush it. It has to be emptied by hand. Dan said, "You're supposed to care about something other than moving through space." I hooked an arm over his shoulder. Earlier that day, over that same shoulder, I'd seen a shirtless man in purple running shorts, whom I wanted to be like. I dropped some words into Dan's ear: "Nothing can be better than being here with you." He kissed my cheek. I didn't flush the way I'd seen his pale boys do. Just as some people use words like "therefore" and "however" but make no argument, this vacant plastic garden lot was circular. The relation-ship opened.

VIII

Dan's hand on his hip. His reddish eyes. Scraggly chest hair he seemed proud of only sometimes. Red plaid curtains in the kitchen on pause. "I just can't, not with you," he said. A contraction happens. It can't not. Naturally, I buckled in my mind, although outside, I was all that the undisturbed lake wants from its surface, without even the echoing when a stone is skipped across.

IX

I paused when Dan wanted to film us going at it then being gone. Dan was also an actor. Porn and non. A streetside tree doesn't lose all its leaves when trucks bump it en route to elsewhere. That was me, in bed. My body bent in ways Dan said to and the camera loved. I was like a river that swells, decimating a local population of one, but in a border town called Machoville. After accessing the footage, I still couldn't see what he did when he looked at me. But his mind, like mine, I thought, must be an engine. Meaning a curb is involved. A stopping place where people in their vehicles don't get hurt.

X

At brunch, over toast, I wanted to show Dan my sketch. In it, a body has been thrown to the earth as a punishment. I copied the body from an old book. In the tale, God's rationale for issuing such a fling job is that truth will spring back out of the earth. I never did show it, lest Dan feel me reaching.

At dinner, in the city's midsection, Dan put his tongue in my ear. Friends in tight tops twittered around the table. Public-facing playacting plus privacy. My mind did go on when it turned. Like a forked road, it's a tongue.

In the back of a midnight cab, my head dropped to his shoulder. My self-talk went along: "Don't be distant or he'll see you leaning backwards, into a pit. That pit is between you and him. Don't look stuck up, like ears. Or cold. Listen for the journey behind his words. Get a glimpse of long train tracks between two mountains, and between the two mountains, down below, you'll see the waters of Averno, clear and circling, that you're both in, trying to get out."

XI

"I'm jerking off," said his text. He meant he was pulling on the one root he has. Neither of us could help but hold unto that.

XII

We were wandering downtown when we hit on an intersection of actors, a crew, and several silver trailers. Dan said, "Isn't the whole plot she doesn't know she's hot?" I fingered a flier. A bird on a powerline doesn't always see its own species around, and *it* isn't disturbed. We weren't either. The actors didn't look at us. Didn't look like either of us. Each actor was a paperclip, like one you unbend with one hand while talking absent-mindedly to someone, say your mother, on the phone.

XIII

We stopped at a pond. The pond didn't stop. In ever-widening circles, green and orange koi fish repeated themselves. They alternated without excluding each other. "It just goes to flow," said Dan, in aviators, on my right. I put my teacher eyes on. Understood, in the substitution, some water in the tap.

XIV

Dan, in his next posted pic, gave himself a smeared set of pecs and the oiled-up, shut-eyed look. I looked up. A man in black leather on a motorcycle was not needing to put either foot down when he slowed at a stop sign then sped up for his turning, which showed off his beefiness that was charity to my eyes. That there was only one man and one bike made no new form in me to level with.

XV

Let's call it chance, that coffee line I landed in with Dan. I wore a blue
backwards baseball cap plus a silver stud. Machoville presumption could
rock me in its arms, as long as Dan's. He reached out to grab the two paper
cups. I couldn't make out the other name. A gleaming, and it came. It was
the perfect boyfriend of Dan, Dan. "O float me, device, down sidewalks," I
almost said. I couldn't talk right then. I was too busy being that concrete.

XVI

Words can't unslurp the hot soup I did, waiting for Dan against one wall. One at a time was my motto. Even a wall can explain this red brick lip. I was intent on thinning out our now infrequent hangouts, like rain drops don't a spider's web. Dan got off his bike. He kicked-split the leg to stand it up. A walk in the park was all I had planned. As if it would de-story me to dare something else. Dan winked.

XVII

Dan and I got on a boat, speeding to some tourist trap alternative. It wasn't like before. I kept flashing to being held by Dan, sometimes down. Just as grapes are purplish only sometimes, the waves broke and were describable. They broke and were. So they had a parallel to instructions I sometimes gave myself: break, describe, break. Dan stuck to his starboard side, on and on his phone. Meanwhile, I was becoming like a complex case of fraud that agrees to be reviewed under the delusion that in so doing, some margin of error might open up. Like a hallway. And at the end of it, a door.

XVIII

Under an umbrella in a plaza, someone was singing to himself. I stopped to catch his unselfconsciousness. Coveted a piece of that action. I exchanged the glances I needed to, to get my fixture of him. He introduced himself as Dario. We strayed to the supermarket, where he worked himself up at a fruit stand. As if plucking a mango from the pile might de-ice him from my friend zone. He squeezed the mango. And I nodded like an outline nods, when a child understands that every color in his picture is a scribbling about belonging. I was drawn to Dario's lack of caution. His red cheeks. My mind started in on spit, from my lips to his.

XIX

On the army-green twin cot in his friend's spot, I spat in Dario's mouth when he motioned me to. Later I went around the neighborhood, counting the cracks in the slabs my feet forwarded over, planning my up and down, my up and down. Every neighborhood sugarcoats its temporariness. I held onto what felt good. Comforted my zone. Typified late solace as something other than my teeth. Some narratives stop short of a sentence.

XX

I stuck words onto silence like pieces of tape.

Dario

hand

waist

"Yeah, put your hand here. Like that." Dario was like Dan, and I was
like myself, and the sun was like the sun when it shadows a tree, and the
shadow wags when a pigeon leaves it, and it leaves me. I had to be someone
about to crash.

XXI

The pink tree in my neighbor's yard confused me. I once did call its pink bits in the wind a spell. Something about wanting a child. But it wasn't, exactly. I pulled on my white cloud jacket and looked at some Dad type two doors down. His right hand was in his pull-over pocket. Some tyke was pulling on his left hand, big eyes on the latest find: a trampoline. When a window slammed, I only supplied, "That's one implacable window." It was inexplicable. I laughed. Something about Dad guy going up steps two at a time made my mouth belong to the yard.

XXII

I pulled off my torso with my thumb and finger. Compare that inch I pinched to the superior packets of artificial sugar I wanted to be to him. Not to last forever. Not to be stored. Not to insist on edibility. Not to back the back of his tongue I pulled on with my tongue, so the spaces widen between syllables. Not to work a caustic clause. Not to miss him and become him. Not to sweeten the increase. Not to confuse the backwaters I was coming from with all salinity.

XXIII

Turning back, on a bridge, Dan faced me. He sighed, a high sound sharpening. I lagged on that stone. He said, "You think you'll reach some pronounceable self-accusation?" It wasn't a question. I was looking for good light to take our portraits in. This became a little rote exercise.

XXIV

Dan once told me, "You only ever think the less that you know." This was when he'd been cutting up an old white shirt to expose more of his wide lats. The whole zigzag.

Dan once told me, "When I feel tense, I feel tragic." He'd been loafing per his usual in the grass, with some distance device-like in devotion. I felt that sky click each time. I felt my quick breath ganging up on my lack of questions, my fingering each temple. The ache became an outline of my head.

XXV

I was flat on my back in bed when my backwardness to history became like a path put down by a public authority, then paved. That naturalness was error, coming back. Like hedges that scratch each other over. When I thought about error, I sometimes thought about parks. It was funding of parks as lately I can't not comment on. Millimeters aren't lackadaisical by force. Keeping my eyes closed, I strolled. Bye everyone! That's why I loved public parks.

XXVI

Dennis, by the piers. Someone had just broken up with him on account of needing more than sex. "More than this," said Dennis, gesturing down to his body. Almost twice the age of mine. He shrugged all over. A mountain. I became other mountains, smaller, yes, but all around a lake, so that when someone shouts, that someone hears their own voice come back in a longer shape. "Wow" and "Damn" flew off my mouth. I admired Dennis for that mad spring sprint, and not doubling back, and this: "I don't worry about losing my attractiveness."

XXVII

My eyes got caught on a glint of his hair. Dennis dyed it whitish, broke it into interlocking segments. Also buzzed the sides to make the thinning top seem less thin. I sometimes wished my hair was like that, if only to seem more of a piece with him. I gripped a railing and turned my feet to the street, went down a brief hill like that, to face the harbor. I was out of touch with the uses of my body. Dennis too. We'd both flung ourselves into so many a bed that we could only climax counterclockwise.

XXVIII

Dennis and I stayed silent for stretches at a time, the way words are when you've rewritten them until what they don't say shines.

XXIX

Inside the movie theater, we assigned ourselves seats for the actual projection of a ray of light. Like flies buzzing on a yellow Sunday. I told myself I only needed the acting. I shifted between Dennis in profile in the seat next to me and men on screen.

XXX

Another plaza. So corporate was this plaza that I understood the installed stone was there for its own purpose. And yet a stone thrown is not its own slowness, was my gander. I kept looking. Water kept falling down the installed face.

XXXI

Dennis pulled up a wicker chair. Over an order of guacamole, he started telling me how, although we do not know the whole story of where we come from, there, in our psyche, a void in the shape of it does exist. No easy essay exit. His father, for example, "underflowed" something "epic" and so endurance comes to be "anyone's." Fear didn't fall through my stomach. Or not at the rate I'd expected. I felt like the construction of men in neon orange vests wiping their foreheads with the softer backs of gloves.

XXXII

I remember Dan's back in the sheer white shirt that he'd let hang down. It was like nothingness met my eyes for not the last time. I watched him go through the front door. Under his arm, a black box of tools. I remember when Dan scooched closer to the chips on a table at the outside cafe, and the sea's air, and how I sucked back my thought. I remember when he'd just met my eyes, how he took one earbud out then flushed a scarlet that doubled as an adrenaline shot to my crotch, which had put him in touch, minus the words, with a cardinal zipping past, abandoning its branch. I remember how he'd introduced himself: "That cardinal you'd compare me to? Don't." Down the stairs Tuesday's shadow fell, in thirds.

XXXIII

We both made gestures at the table. Each gesture was like that of an actor whose eyes shine and who raises his voice, or lets it die, in a performance to watch later on repeat. A waiter came and went, came and went, with margaritas. My eyes met his then those of the man across from me, in his ribbed velcro affair. I looked and looked even after my sight went away. I didn't share that in the almost purplish infant light, evening was a leap. I stayed in the feeling of the shoes on my feet. My hand on my lap. I was a believer, in the cold, in saying one thing inside and another outside.

Coda

No one can be all the words they are to themselves. No one can be all the words. They are to themselves.

My hand crosses the page. Back and forth stays one same sane. The body times three. Although the body serves me, and me it, and the body can betray, still they go together: my notebook bore love poems. I could be shy about them, or not.

Notes

"Of His Mistrisse upon Occasion of Her Walking in a Garden" draws upon Elaine Scarry's argument about the identity of Shakespeare's beloved as outlined in her book *Naming Thy Name: Cross Talk in Shakespeare's Sonnets*.

"A Visit to Hades" is an ekphrastic response to the gay pornography film *What I Can't See* by Treasure Island Media, an early film featuring condomless sex in the era of HIV/AIDS.

"Teotihuacan and Us" is an ekphrastic response to Paige Jiyoung Moon's painting of the same name, acrylic on canvas, 20 x 16 inches.

"The Leniad" includes a passage from Mary Jo Bang's translation of Dante's *Inferno* as well as a line from Tory Dent's "R.I.P., My Love" in her collection *HIV, Mon Amour* ("What I'm trying to say is that it wasn't lonely.") The prose blocks in "The Leniad" catalog each appearance of the eyes, the heart, grief, men, the mind, night, sleep, wind, and words as metaphors in Emily Wilson's translation of *The Odyssey*. Leni: "I paraphrased them radically."

"Virgil" includes an excerpt of *The Aeneid* translated by Shadi Bartsch, lines 273-281 in Book 5, where Aeneas and his crew have just left for the sea, leaving Dido behind.

"Machoville" draws on Allen Mandelbaum's translation of Dante's *Inferno*, *Purgatorio*, and *Paradiso*. This piece also draws on interviews with visual artists and writers Claudia Rankine, Cecily Brown, Dennis Cooper, Deborah Eisenberg, and Lynette Yiadom-Boakye.

Acknowledgments

Thanks to the editors of the following publications for publishing some of these poems:

Granta
"The Second He"

The Harvard Advocate
"Another Swan"
"Hoping for an Opening"

Neon Door
"Ovid"
"Teotihuacan and Us"

Peste Magazine
"Sappho"
"Virgil"
"[A scant metaphysics]" from "The Leniad"
"[Blowback]" from "The Leniad"
"[A man is a force, but feeling...]" from "The Leniad"
"[Doing love well is will]" from "The Leniad"
"[He's aware]" from "The Leniad"
"[He's not mine. Nor are his hands]" from "The Leniad"

New American Writing
"Byzantium"
"Dead Would"

Rogue Agent
"Machoville XXI"

Second Factory
"It Happens, So I Fall"

Subtropics
"About Being Cold"
"Of His Mistrisse upon Occasion of Her Walking in a Garden"

Superstition Review
"Machoville I"
"Machoville II"
"Machoville III"
"Machoville IV"
"Machoville V"
"Machoville VI"
"Machoville VII"

Thanks as well to the editors of *Fives: a Companion to the Denver Quarterly* for publishing "Availability makes him often gathering" and "What I'm trying to say is that it wasn't lonely," two collages by James Scales from his collage sequence that illustrates "The Leniad."

Thanks to Aaron Kent and the team at Broken Sleep Books for recognizing and believing in this manuscript and for making the object of it so beautiful. And to Andre Bagoo, for lending an ear. And to James Scales, Kelsey Peterson, Natasha Yglesias, and Poupeh Missaghi for the clear-eyed feedback that guided me through assembling this book.

LAY OUT YOUR UNREST